SOCK YARN SCARVES

by Knit Picks

Printed in the United States of America

First Printing, 2014

ISBN 978-1-62767-054-8

Versa Press, Inc
800-447-7829

www.versapress.com

CONTENTS

RIDGE AND ARROW

by Courtney Spainhower

FINISHED MEASUREMENTS
72" circumference, 12" wide at widest point

YARN
Knit Picks Stroll Sock Yarn (75% Superwash Merino Wool, 25% Nylon; 231 yards/50g): Dogwood Heather 25603, 3 balls.

NEEDLES
US 6 (4mm) straight or circular needles, or size to obtain gauge

NOTIONS
Yarn Needle
Scrap yarn

Size H Crochet hook
Spare DPNs

GAUGE
24 sts and 32 rows = 4" over Stockinette, blocked.
26 sts and 40 rows = 4" in Heel stitch, blocked.
20 sts and 28 rows = 4" in Arrow Lace pattern, blocked. (Gauge for this project is approximate)

Ridge and Arrow

Notes:

Provisional Cast-on
Using scrap yarn and a crochet hook, create a chain a few stitches longer than the number of stitches you will be casting on. Pick up and knit cast-on stitches through the bumps to the back of the chain using the working yarn for the pattern.

Kitchener Stitch
Holding the two pieces to be grafted parallel with wrong sides touching, thread yarn needle with the long tail and set up for joining. *Insert the yarn needle knit-wise into the first stitch on the front knitting needle, draw through the stitch and slip the stitch off of the front needle. Insert the yarn needle purl-wise into the next stich on the front knitting needle, draw through the stitch leaving the stitch on the needle. Insert the yarn needle purl-wise into the first stitch on the back knitting needle, draw through the stitch and slip the stitch off of the back needle. Insert the yarn needle knit-wise into the next stitch on the back knitting needle, draw through the stitch leaving the stitch on the needle. Repeat these steps beginning at * until all of your stitches have been grafted together.

Heel Stitch (worked flat over an even number of sts)
Row 1 (RS): Sl1pw, *K1, Sl1kw; repeat from * to last stitch, K1.

Row 2 (WS): Sl1pw, Purl to end.

Repeat rows 1 and 2 for pattern.

Arrow Lace Pattern (worked flat over multiple of 18 + 1 sts)
Row 1 (RS): K5, K2tog *yo, K1, yo, K3, yo, K1, yo, ssk, K9, K2tog; repeat from* to last 12 sts, yo, K1, yo, K3, yo, K1, yo, ssk, K5.

Row 2 (WS): P4, P2tog tbl *P9, P2tog, P7, P2tog tbl; repeat from* to last 15 sts, P9, P2tog, P4.

Row 3: K3, K2tog *(yo, K3) 3 times, yo, ssk, K5, K2tog; repeat from* to last 15 sts, (yo, K3) 3 times, yo, ssk, K3.

Row 4: P2, P2tog tbl *P13, P2tog, P3, P2tog tbl; repeat from * to last 17sts, P13, P2tog, P2.

Row 5: K1, K2tog *yo, K5, yo, K3, yo, K5, yo, ssk, K1, K2tog; repeat from* to last 16 sts, yo, K5, yo, K3, yo, K5, yo, ssk, K1.

Row 6: P2tog *P17, P3tog; repeat from * to last 19 sts, P17, P2tog tbl.

Row 7: K2, yo, K1, yo *ssk, K9, K2tog, yo, K1, yo, K3, yo, K1, yo; repeat from * to last 16 sts, ssk, K9, K2tog, yo, K1, yo, K2.

Row 8: P5 *P2tog, P7, P2tog tbl, P9; repeat from *   to last 16 sts, P2tog, P7, P2tog tbl, P5.

Row 9: K2, yo, K3, yo *ssk, K5, K2tog, (yo, K3) 3 times, yo; repeat from * to last 14 sts, ssk, K5, K2tog, yo, K3, yo, K2.

Row 10: P7 *P2tog, P3, P2tog tbl, P13; repeat from * to last 14 sts, P2tog, P3, P2tog tbl, P7.

Row 11: K2, yo, K5, yo *ssk, K1, K2tog, yo, K5, yo, K3, yo, K5, yo; repeat from * to last 12 sts, ssk, K1, K2tog, yo, K5, yo, K2.

Row 12: P9 *P3tog, P17; repeat from * to last 12 sts, P3tog, P9.

Repeat Rows 1-12 for pattern.

DIRECTIONS
Using Provisional Cast-on method, CO 54 sts.

Purl 1 row.

Begin working Heel stitch, repeating rows 1 and 2 a total of 150 times (about 30").

Knit 1 row increasing as follows: K27, M1, K27 (55 sts).

Purl 1 row, then begin Arrow Lace.

Repeat rows 1-12 of Arrow Lace Pattern a total of 17 times.

On row 12 of final repeat, work as follows: P9 *P3tog, P17; repeat from * to last 12 sts, P4tog, P8 (54 sts).

Break yarn leaving an 18" tail but do not bind-off.

Place stitches onto scrap yarn and move on to finishing.

Finishing
Wash and block to diagram.

Remove scrap yarn from Cast-on and from end stitches transferring them onto double-pointed needles to prepare for grafting.

Using Kitchener Stitch, graft stitches together and weave in ends.

GRADIENT WAVES COWL

by Hope Vickman

FINISHED MEASUREMENTS
22.25" (56.5cm) circumference x 8.5" (21.5cm) high

YARN
Knit Picks Comfy Fingering (75% Pima Cotton, 25% Acrylic; 218 yards/50g):
MC: Douglas Fir 25761, 1 ball.
CC: Peapod 24830, 1 ball.

NEEDLES
US 0 (2.00mm) 16" (40cm) circular needles, or one size smaller than needles used to obtain gauge

US 1 (2.50mm) 16" (40cm) circular needles, or size to obtain gauge

NOTIONS
Yarn Needle
Stitch Markers

GAUGE
32 sts and 36 rows = 4" (10cm) over stranded colorwork using larger sized needles, blocked.

Gradient Waves Cowl

Notes:

This cowl is knit in the round using stranded colorwork. The top and bottom edges have a Seed stitch border in the Main Color only. The middle section of the cowl is knit using the chart provided. The chart is 178 sts long and has a 16 round repeat. Follow the chart from bottom (round 1) to top reading every row from right to left.

M1L (Make 1 Left-leaning stitch)

PU the bar between st just worked and next st and place on LH needle as a regular stitch; knit through the back of the loop.

DIRECTIONS

With smaller sized needles and MC yarn, cast on 177 sts. Place marker and join to work in the round (being careful not to twist sts).

Bottom Border

Round 1: *K1, P1* repeat around to 1 stitch before marker. K1, slip marker.

Round 2: *P1, K1* repeat around to 1 stitch before marker. P1, slip marker.

Rounds 3-8: Repeat Rounds 1 & 2 another 3 times.

Round 9: Repeat Round 1 once more.

Round 10: Repeat Round 2 until 1 stitch before marker. P1, M1L, slip marker. (178 sts)

Body of Cowl

Switch to larger sized needles.

Knitting all sts for all rounds, join CC yarn and begin working from charted directions.

Repeat the 16 charted rounds until the cowl measures approximately 7.25" (18.5 cm) or 0.75" (2cm) less than desired height.

Top Border

Next Round: Break CC yarn. Using MC yarn only, K2tog, then K to the end of the round. (177 sts)

Switch to smaller sized needles.

Round 1: *K1, P1* repeat around to 1 stitch before marker, K1, slip marker.

Round 2: *P1, K1* repeat around to 1 stitch before marker, P1, slip marker.

Rounds 3-10: Repeat rounds 1 & 2 another 4 times.

Bind-off all stitches in pattern.

Finishing

Weave in ends, wash and block to measurements.

Gradient Chart

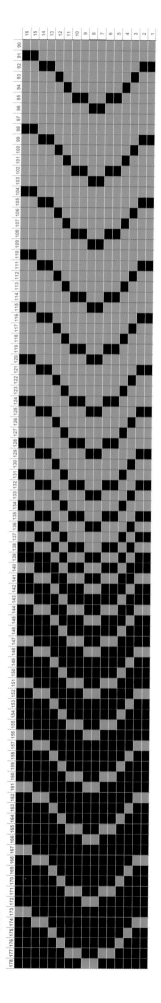

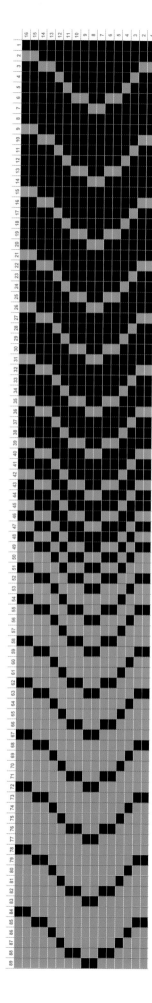

Legend

BEES AND HONEYBEES WRAP

by Stephanie Tallent

FINISHED MEASUREMENTS

8.25" wide, 80" long

YARN

Knit Picks Stroll Sock Yarn (75% Superwash Merino, 25% Nylon; 231 yds/50gm): Dandelion 25024, 3 balls

NEEDLES

US 3 (3mm) straight needles or 24" or longer circular needles, or size to obtain gauge

NOTIONS

Yarn Needle

Scrap Yarn, Stitch Holders, or Spare Needle

GAUGE

Approx 33 sts and 32 rows = 4" in Main Repeat pattern, blocked.

For pattern support, contact sunset.cat.designs@gmail.com

Bees and Honeybees Wrap

Notes:

The scarf is knit in two halves and grafted in the middle. There are several good tutorials on how to work the Kitchener stitch when not all of the sts are knitted. A great one from Knitty is here: http://www.knitty.com/ISSUEw12/PATTrime.php (scroll down).

The Honeybee Lace pattern is created by dropping yarnover(s) made on the 2nd, 3rd, 4th, and 5th rows of the six-row repeat and then gathering the dropped strands on the 6th row with the Honey Bee Knit stitch. Yarn overs are dropped in the Honeybee Lace sections ONLY.

Honeybee Lace pattern (9 – 13 sts and 6 rows – worked flat)
Row 1 (WS): P5, P2tog, P6.

Row 2 (RS): K4, K2tog, YO, SSK, K4.

Row 3: P3, SSP, YO 2 times, drop yo from previous row, P2tog, P3.

Row 4: K2, K2tog, YO 3 times, drop yo's from previous row, SSK, K2.

Row 5: P1, SSP, YO 4 times, drop yo's from previous row, P2tog, P1.

Row 6: K2tog, CO 4, drop yo's from previous row, HB, YO, HB, CO 4, SSK. (Cast on sts using backwards loop method.)

HB (Honeybee Knit Stitch)
Place needle under dropped yarnovers from the 4 previous rows. K1 under the 4 loose strands.

DIRECTIONS

CO 87 sts.

Setup Row (WS): Knit across.Rows 1 – 25: Work Set Up Chart. Note that the chart ends with a RS row.

Begin working Main Repeat Chart. Note that the chart begins on a WS row.

Work 22 repeats of the Main Chart, ending with a Row 12. Place stitches on waste yarn, a stitch holder or a spare needle. Set aside.

Repeat for second half.

Finishing

Graft both halves of the scarf together such that the purl columns are purled and the remainder of the stitches are grafted with knit stitches.

Weave in all ends. Block lightly.

Main Repeat

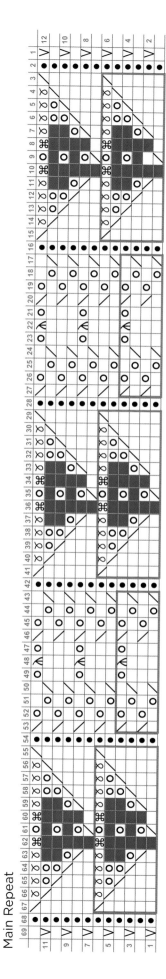

Set Up Chart

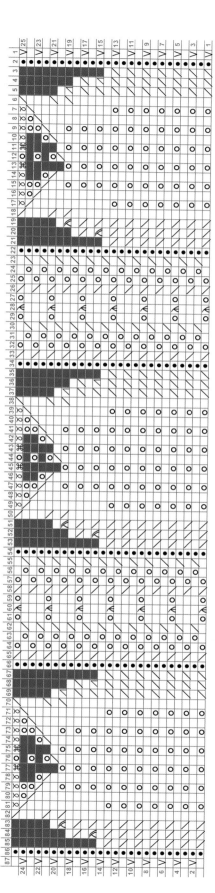

Legend

knit
RS: knit stitch
WS: purl stitch

• **purl**
RS: purl stitch
WS: knit stitch

◹ **k2tog**
RS: Knit two stitches together as one stitch
WS: Purl 2 stitches together

■ **No Stitch**
RS: Placeholder - No stitch made.

○ **YO**
Yarn Over

Ⅴ **slip**
RS: Slip stitch as if to purl, holding yarn in back
WS: Slip stitch as if to purl, holding yarn in front

◺ **ssk**
RS: Slip one stitch as if to knit, Slip another stitch as if to knit. Insert left-hand needle into front of these 2 stitches and knit them together
WS: Purl two stitches together in back loops, inserting needle from the left, behind and into the backs of the 2nd & 1st stitches in that order

⋏ **sl1 k2tog psso**
RS: slip 1, k2tog, pass slip stitch over k2tog

⊗ **CO**
Cast on one stitch

⌘ **Honeybee Knit Stitch**
Place needle under dropped yarnovers from the 4 previous rows. K1 under the 4 loose strands.

□ **Pattern Repeats**

◹ **k3tog**
RS: Knit three stitches together as one
WS: Purl three stitches together as one

ⴥ **sssk**
RS: (Slip 1 as if to knit) 3 times; insert left-hand needle from the front to the back of all stitches at the same time and knit them together.
WS: (Slip 1 as if to knit) 3 times; insert left-hand needle from the front to the back of all stitches at the same time and knit them together.

EVERLASTING COWL

by Robin Allen

FINISHED MEASUREMENTS

8" (20 cm) high; 25" (63.5 cm) circumference

YARN

Knit Picks Stroll Glimmer Yarn (70% Fine Superwash Merino Wool, 25% Nylon, 5% Stellina; 231 yards/50g): Kestrel 26085, 1 ball.

NEEDLES

US 3 (3.25mm) 24" or shorter circular needle, or size to obtain gauge

NOTIONS

Yarn Needle
Stitch Markers

GAUGE

22 sts and 32 rows = 4" in Everlasting Lace pattern, blocked and relaxed. (Gauge for this project is approximate.)

Everlasting Cowl

Notes:

This feminine cowl uses a stitch pattern of yesterday on the accessory of today. Knit seamlessly in the round using knits, purls, yarn over increases, and decreases, it's a satisfying lacy little knit.

Seed Stitch
*K1, P1; rep from * to end of round.

Everlasting Lace (worked over multiples of 14 sts)
Round 1: *K1, YO, K1, YO, K2, P3, P3tog, P3, K1; rep from * to end of round.

Round 2: *K6, P7, K1; rep from * to end of round.

Round 3: *K1, YO, K3, YO, K2, P2, P3tog, P2, K1; rep from * to end of round.

Round 4: *K8, P5, K1; rep from * to end of round.

Round 5: *K1, YO, K5, YO, K2, P1, P3tog, P1, K1; rep from * to end of round.

Round 6: *K10, P3, K1; rep from * to end of round.

Round 7: *K1, YO, K7, YO, K2, P3tog, K1; rep from * to end of round.

Round 8: *K12, P1, K1; rep from * to end of round.

Round 9: *K1, P3, P3tog, P3, K2, YO, K1, YO, K1; rep from * to end of round.

Round 10: *K1, P7, K6; rep from * to end of round.

Round 11: *K1, P2, P3tog, P2, K2, YO, K3, YO, K1; rep from * to end of round.

Round 12: *K1, P5, K8; rep from * to end of round.

Round 13: *K1, P1, P3tog, P1, K2, YO, K5, YO, K1; rep from * to end of round.

Round 14: *K1, P3, K10; rep from * to end of round.

Round 15: *K1, P3tog, K2, YO, K7, YO, K1; rep from * to end of round.

Round 16: *K1, P1, K12; rep from * to end of round.

Directions

Loosely CO 140 sts. PM and join for working in the round, being careful not to twist the line of sts.

Work 1 round in Seed stitch.

Knit 1 round, placing markers every 14 sts.

Work rounds 1–16 of Everlasting Lace 3 times, using chart or written instructions. Work each line of instructions, or row of the chart, 10 times across each round.

Knit 1 round, removing all but beg of rnd marker.

Work 1 round in Seed stitch.

Finishing

Loosely BO all sts. Weave in ends and block to measurements.

Everlasting Lace Chart

18	17	16	15	14	13	12	11	10	9	8	7	6	5	4	3	2	1	
												●		█	█	█	█	16
	O								O			◹			█	█	█	15
█											●	●	●		█	█	█	14
█		O						O			●	◹	●			█	█	13
█	█									●	●	●	●				█	12
█			O				O			●	●	◹	●				█	11
█									●	●	●	●	●	●				10
█	█	█	O		O				●	●	●	◹	●	●	●		9
█	█	█			●													8
█	█	█			◹			O							O			7
█	█	█		●	●	●												6
█	█			●	◹	●			O					O				5
█			●	●	●	●	●								█	█		4
█			●	●	◹	●	●		O				O			█		3
█		●	●	●	●	●	●	●									█	2
█		●	●	●	◹	●	●	●			O		O					1

Legend

█	No Stitch	placeholder - no stitch made
☐	knit	knit stitch
O	YO	yarn over
●	purl	purl stitch
◹	p3tog	purl three stitches together as one

ESTIVATE

by Teresa Gregorio

FINISHED MEASUREMENTS

S (M, L, XL): 43 (50, 59, 69.25) bottom opening circumference; garment is meant to be worn with approximately 8" of positive ease.

27.75 (28.5, 29.25, 29.75)" neck opening circumference; 14 (15, 17, 18)" long.

YARN

Knit Picks Stroll Tonal Sock (75% Superwash Merino Wool, 25% Nylon; 462 yards/100g): Springtime 24910 3 (3, 4, 4) hanks.

NEEDLES

US 4 (3.5mm) 24" or longer circular needles, or size to obtain gauge.

NOTIONS

Yarn Needle
Stitch Markers
Crochet Hook (for provisional CO)
Smooth Waste Yarn (for provisional CO)
Scrap yarn or stitch holders.

GAUGE

21 sts and 32 rows = 4" over Vine Lace pattern, blocked.

Estivate

Notes:

Estivate is a convertible scarf/bolero that's airy enough to be your summer's constant companion, whether after the sun goes down around the campfire, or as a pretty accessory added to your formal outfit for those summer weddings. Knit in the shape of a large rectangle, Estivate uses provisional cast ons, worked from the bottom front edge up, and then grafted at the bottom edges to create a smoothly joined tube.

Vine Lace (worked flat over a multiple of 9 + 4 sts)

Rows 1 and 3 (WS): Purl.

Row 2 (RS): K3, *yo, k2, ssk, k2tog, k2, yo, k1* rep from * to * to one st before end, k1.

Row 4 (RS): K2, *yo, k2, ssk, k2tog, k2, yo, k1* rep from * to * to two sts before end, k2.

Repeat Rows 1-4 for pattern.

Provisional Cast On (Crochet Chain Method)

Using a crochet hook several sizes too big for the yarn, make a loose chain of about six stitches more than you need to cast on. Cut yarn and pull tail through last chain. With a knitting needle and your working yarn, beginning two stitches from last chain worked, pick up and knit one stitch through the back loop of each chain for desired number of stitches.

To unravel when sts need to be picked up, pull out the crochet chain, leaving live sts.

Cable Cast On

Make a slip knot and place it on the LH needle. Knit into this st, and slip this new st onto the LH needle pwise. *Insert the tip of your right needle between the two sts on your left needle. Wrap the yarn around and draw a loop through. Insert your left needle tip into this loop from right to left and remove your right needle from the st. Repeat from * until the required number of sts are on the needle, lightly tightening the sts as you go along.

Kitchener Stitch (grafting)

With an equal number of stitches on two needles, break yarn leaving several feet of tail and thread through yarn needle. Hold needles parallel, with WS's facing in and both needles pointing to the right. Perform Step 2 on the first front st, and then Step 4 on the first back st, and then continue with instructions below.

1: Pull yarn needle kwise through front stitch and drop stitch from knitting needle.

2: Pull yarn needle pwise through next front stitch, leave stitch on knitting needle.

3: Pull yarn needle pwise through first back stitch and drop stitch from knitting needle.

4: Pull yarn needle kwise through next back stitch, leave stitch on knitting needle.

Repeat steps 1 – 4 until all stitches have been grafted.

If you are unsure of how to work the cast ons, Knit Picks has demonstrational videos with two different types of provisional cast ons, and the Cabled cast on: The Traditional Provisional (http://tutorials.knitpicks.com/wptutorials/traditional-provisional/), the Crocheted Provisional (http://tutorials.knitpicks.com/wptutorials/crocheted-provisional-cast-on/), and the Cabled cast on (http://tutorials.knitpicks.com/wptutorials/cabled-cast-on/).

Grafting, also called the Kitchener Stitch, is demonstrated in Knit Pick's video here (http://tutorials.knitpicks.com/wptutorials/kitchener-stitch/).

DIRECTIONS

Front

Using a provisional cast on, CO 60 (60, 66, 66) sts, using Cable Cast On CO 113 (131, 155, 182) sts, then provisionally cast on 60 (60, 66, 66) sts. 233 (251, 287, 314) sts.

Row 1 (WS): Sl 1, k1, pm, p to 2 sts before end, pm, k2.

Row 2 (RS): Sl 1, k1, sm, work in Vine Lace to marker, sm, k2.

Row 3 (WS): Sl 1, k1, sm, work in Vine Lace to marker, sm, k2.

Rep Rows 2 and 3 while working the 4-row Vine Lace pat repeats, until piece measures 13 (14, 16, 17)" or desired length, ending on RS Row 4 of Vine Lace.

Creating the Neckline

Row 1 (WS): K first 80 (88, 105, 118) sts, bind off next 73 (75, 77, 78) sts, k rem 80 (88, 105, 118) sts.

Row 2 (RS): K first 80 (88, 105, 118) sts, Cable Cast On 73 (75, 77, 78) sts, k rem 80 (88, 105, 118) sts.

For a narrower neckline, BO fewer sts on Row 1 and then CO an amount equal to the BO sts on Row 2. Each 10 st reduction will reduce the circumference by approx. 2" at the given gauge.

Back

Row 1 (WS): Sl 1, k1, sm, work in Vine Lace to marker, sm, k2.

Row 2 (RS): Sl 1, k1, sm, work in Vine Lace to marker, sm, k2.

Rep Rows 1 and 2 as est for Front until piece measures 13 (14, 16, 17)" or desired length to match Front, ending on RS Row 4 of Vine Lace.

Break yarn.

Binding Off

Place first 60 (60, 66, 66) sts on scrap yarn. Reattach yarn. Bind off next 113 (131, 155, 182). Break yarn. Place rem 60 (60, 66, 66) sts on scrap yarn.

Finishing

Weave in ends. Wash and block to Finished Measurements. Unravel the provisionally cast on sts and place resulting live sts on needles. Graft the Front and Back sts tog along the bottom edge.

Weave in remaining ends.

SIEMPRE

by Kristen Jancuk

FINISHED MEASUREMENTS

6" high, 48" circumference

YARN

Knit Picks Stroll Glimmer (70% Fine Superwash Merino Wool, 25% Nylon, 5% Stellina; 231 yards/50g): Runway 25490, 2 balls.

NEEDLES

US 3 (3.25mm) straight or circular needles, or size to obtain gauge

NOTIONS

Yarn Needle
Stitch Markers
Crochet Hook for Provisional Cast On
Cable Needle
Smooth Scrap Yarn for Provisional Cast On

GAUGE

30 sts and 40 rows = 4" in Chart A lace pattern, blocked.

Siempre

Notes:

This infinity scarf is knit flat from a provisional cast on, then the live stitches are grafted to form a loop.

Chart A, Written Directions

Row 1 (RS): K7, K2tog, K6, double YO, K6, Ssk, K7.

Row 2 (WS): P14, K1, K1 tbl (in second YO), P14.

Row 3: K6, K2tog, K6, YO, P2, YO, K6, Ssk, K6.

Rows 4, 6, 8, 10, 12, 14, 16, 18 and 20: P13, K4, P13.

Row 5: K5, K2tog, K6, YO, P4, YO, K6, Ssk, K5.

Row 7: K4, K2tog, K6, YO, K1, P4, K1, YO, K6, Ssk, K4.

Row 9: K3, K2tog, K6, YO, K2, P4, K2, YO, K6, Ssk, K3.

Row 11: K2, K2tog, K6, YO, K3, P4, K3, YO, K6, Ssk, K2.

Row 13: K1, K2tog, K6, YO, K4, P4, K4, YO, K6, Ssk, K1.

Row 15: K2tog, K6, YO, K5, P4, K5, YO, K6, Ssk.

Row 17: Ssk, K1, YO, K10, P4, K10, YO, K1, K2tog.

Row 19: K1, Ssk, K1, YO, K9, P4, K9, YO, K1, K2tog, K1.

Chart B, Written Directions

Row 1 (RS): K9, C6B, C6F, K9.

Rows 2, 4, 6, 8 (WS): P30.

Row 3: K6, C6B, K6, C6F, K6.

Row 5: K3, C6B, K12, C6F, K3.

Row 7: C6B, K18, C6F.

Right leaning cable (C6B)

Sl 3 sts to CN and hold at back, k3, k3 from CN.

Left leaning cable (C6F)

Sl 3 sts to CN and hold at front, k3, k3 from CN.

Right Twist (RT)

K2tog, leaving sts on left needle; knit into first st again, and slip both sts off needle.

Left Twist (LT)

K 2nd st on left needle through the back loop, then K first st, slipping both sts off needle.

Provisional Cast On

With smooth scrap yarn, crochet a chain several stitches longer than the number of cast on stitches. Using working yarn and given CO needle size, pick up and knit one stitch in the back of each 'bump' of the crochet chain for the given number of CO stitches.

Kitchener Stitch

With an equal number of stitches on two needles, break yarn leaving several feet of tail and thread through tapestry needle. Hold needles parallel, and both needles pointing to the right. Perform Step 2 on the first front st, and then Step 4 on the first back st, and then continue on to Step 1 of instructions below.

1: Pull tapestry needle k-wise through front stitch and drop stitch from knitting needle.

2: Pull tapestry needle p-wise through next front stitch and leave stitch on knitting needle.

3: Pull tapestry needle p-wise through first back stitch and drop stitch from knitting needle.

4: Pull tapestry needle k-wise through next back stitch and leave stitch on knitting needle.

Repeat steps 1 - 4 until all stitches have been grafted.

DIRECTIONS

Using either the suggested or your preferred provisional cast on method, cast on 52 stitches.

Set up row (WS): Sl 1, p2, k3, p2, k3, pm, p30, pm, k3, p2, k3, p3.

Row 1 (RS): Sl 1, k2, p3, RT, p3, sm, work Row 1 of Chart A to next marker, sm, p3, LT, p3, k3.

Row 2 (WS): Sl 1, p2, k3, p2, k3, sm, work Row 2 of Chart A to next marker, sm, k3, p2, k3, p3.

Row 3: Sl 1, k2, p3, k2, p3, sm, work Row 3 of Chart A to next marker, sm, p3, k2, p3, k3.

Row 4: Sl 1, p2, k3, p2, k3, sm, work Row 4 of Chart A to next marker, sm, k3, p2, k3, p3.

Continue to work rows 5-20 of Chart A between markers, working remaining sts as established with RT and LT worked every other RS row as established.

Once one repeat of Chart A is complete, switch to Chart B for stitches between markers, maintaining pattern for remaining sts. Work 2 repeats of Rows 1-8 of Chart B.

After 2 repeats of Chart B are complete, work one repeat of Chart A between markers as established, followed by 3 repeats of Chart B.

Continue as established, alternating 2 and then 3 repeats of Chart B between single repeats of Chart A, until scarf reaches approximately 48" or desired length, ending with a 3rd repeat of Chart B.

Leave live stitches on needle.

Finishing

Unravel the provisionally cast on sts and place resulting live sts on a needle. Using Kitchener Stitch, join cast on stitches with live stitches from end of scarf, being careful to match tension of existing sts.

Weave in ends, wash and block to finished measurements.

Chart A

Columns: 30 29 28 27 26 25 24 23 22 21 20 19 18 17 16 15 14 13 12 11 10 9 8 7 6 5 4 3 2 1

Rows (left): 20 18 16 14 12 10 8 6 4 2
Rows (right): 19 17 15 13 11 9 7 5 3 1

Chart B

Columns: 30 29 28 27 26 25 24 23 22 21 20 19 18 17 16 15 14 13 12 11 10 9 8 7 6 5 4 3 2 1

Rows (left): 8 6 4 2
Rows (right): 7 5 3 1

Legend

knit
RS: knit stitch
WS: purl stitch

k2tog
RS: Knit two stitches together as one stitch
WS: Purl 2 stitches together

O   YO
RS: Yarn Over
WS: Yarn Over

ssk
RS: Slip one stitch as if to knit, Slip another stitch as if to knit. Insert left-hand needle into front of these 2 stitches and knit them together

WS: Purl two stitches together in back loops, inserting needle from the left, behind and into the backs of the 2nd & 1st stitches in that order

B   knit tbl
Knit stitch through back loop

•   purl
RS: purl stitch
WS: knit stitch

C6B
sl3 to CN, hold in back. k3, then k3 from CN

C6F
sl3 to CN, hold in front. k3, k3 from CN

RIDGELINE TRAIL COWL

by Angela Modzelewski

FINISHED MEASUREMENTS

9.5" front center height; 26" lower and 18" upper circumference

YARN

Knit Picks Comfy Fingering (75% Pima Cotton, 25% Acrylic; 218 yards/50g): Ivory 24814, 2 ball

NEEDLES

US 4 (3.5mm) DPNs or 16" circular needles, or size to obtain gauge

NOTIONS

Yarn Needle
Stitch Markers

GAUGE

24 sts and 40 rows = 4" in St st, blocked.

Ridgeline Trail Cowl

Notes:

The Ridgeline Trail Cowl is a bandana or kerchief shaped cowl named after a popular hiking trail in Eugene, Oregon. The ridge design used in the pattern not only creates texture, it makes this project the perfect traveling companion. It's simple to keep track of which row you're on, and the pattern is easy to memorize, yet interesting to knit.

Because it's knit in Comfy, this cowl is soft and easy care. It's fashionable, functional, and fun to knit.

Decrease Round
P to 2 sts before marker, P2tog, SM, K5, SM, P2tog, P to end of round. (2 sts dec).

Cowl Decrease Pattern
Rounds 1 and 2: Work a Decrease Round.

Round 3-5: Knit.

Round 6: Work a Decrease Round.

Rounds 7-9: Knit.

Round 10: Work a Decrease Round.

Rounds 11-13: Knit.

Repeat Rounds 1 through 13 for pattern. 8 sts dec.

DIRECTIONS

CO 156 sts. PM and join in the round. Be careful not to twist the stitches.

Round 1: P78, YO, P78. (157 sts)

Round 2: P78, K1, P78.

Rounds 3-5: K all sts.

Round 6: P75, PM, P2tog, K3, P2tog, PM, P75. (155 sts)

Rounds 7-9: K all sts.

Round 10: Work a Decrease Round. (153 sts)

Rounds 11-13: K all sts.

Rounds 14-78: Work Decrease Pattern 5 times. (113 sts)

Rounds 79, 80: Work a Decrease Round. (109 sts)

Rounds 81-83: K all sts.

Round 84: P48, K5, P48.

Rounds 85-87: K all sts.

Rounds 88-91: Rep Rounds 84-87.

Rounds 92, 93: Rep Round 84.

BO off all stitches loosely in pattern.

Finishing
Weave in ends, wash and block.

Abbreviations

BO	bind off	**M**	marker		stitch	**TBL**	through back loop
cn	cable needle	**M1**	make one stitch	**RH**	right hand	**TFL**	through front loop
CC	contrast color	**M1L**	make one left-leaning	**rnd(s)**	round(s)	**tog**	together
CDD	Centered double dec		stitch	**RS**	right side	**W&T**	wrap & turn (see
CO	cast on	**M1R**	make one right-lean-	**Sk**	skip		specific instructions
cont	continue		ing stitch	**Sk2p**	sl 1, k2tog, pass		in pattern)
dec	decrease(es)	**MC**	main color		slipped stitch over	**WE**	work even
DPN(s)	double pointed	**P**	purl		k2tog: 2 sts dec	**WS**	wrong side
	needle(s)	**P2tog**	purl 2 sts together	**SKP**	sl, k, psso: 1 st dec	**WYIB**	with yarn in back
EOR	every other row	**PM**	place marker	**SL**	slip	**WYIF**	with yarn in front
inc	increase	**PFB**	purl into the front and	**SM**	slip marker	**YO**	yarn over
K	knit		back of stitch	**SSK**	sl, sl, k these 2 sts tog		
K2tog	knit two sts together	**PSSO**	pass slipped stitch	**SSP**	sl, sl, p these 2 sts tog		
KFB	knit into the front and		over		tbl		
	back of stitch	**PU**	pick up	**SSSK**	sl, sl, sl, k these 3 sts		
K-wise	knitwise	**P-wise**	purlwise		tog		
LH	left hand	**rep**	repeat	**St st**	stockinette stitch		
		Rev St st	reverse stockinette	**sts**	stitch(es)		

Knit Picks yarn is both luxe and affordable—a seeming contradiction trounced! But it's not just about the pretty colors; we also care deeply about fiber quality and fair labor practices, leaving you with a gorgeously reliable product you'll turn to time and time again.

THIS COLLECTION FEATURES

Stroll Sock Yarn
Fingering Weight
75% Superwash Merino Wool,
25% Nylon

Comfy
Fingering Weight
75% Pima Cotton, 25% Acrylic

Stroll Tonal Sock
Fingering Weight
75% Superwash Merino Wool,
25% Nylon

Stroll Glimmer
Fingering Weight
75% Superwash Merino Wool,
25% Nylon, 5% Stellina

View these beautiful yarns and
more at www.KnitPicks.com